My Amazing Toddler Behavioral Series

I Stay With My GROWN-UP!

Gentle Affirmations About Safety and Strangers

By Suzanne T. Christian

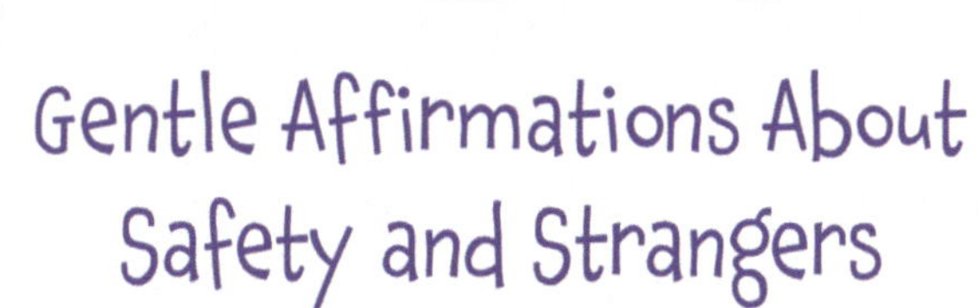

TWORAVENS
BOOKS

Two Little Ravens

CHILDREN'S NON-FICTION BOOKS

Paperback Edition: 9781968080617
Hardcover Edition: 9781968080624
Digital Edition: 9781968080631

Published in the United States by Two Ravens Books LLC,
254 Chapman Rd, Ste 209, Newark DE 19702

'Expand the mind, free the imagination, one title at a time.'
www.tworavensbooks.com

Welcome to
"I Stay With My Grown-Up!"

This book offers gentle affirmations to help young children learn about safety and strangers in a calm way. As you read together, your child will practice staying close to a trusted grown-up, asking before going anywhere, and making safe choices in places like stores, parks, and parking lots.

Each page shows familiar situations, uses comforting words, and offers guidance to help your child feel confident. The lessons are easy to remember and use. This book isn't a quick fix; real growth takes time, patience, and practice. Reading these affirmations often can help your toddler feel more confident, secure, and ready for new experiences.

Add this book to your daily reading routine. Read it with your child each day, and pause to discuss the messages. Use the book to regularly practice safety and connection, helping your child build lasting confidence and comfort.

I hope this book inspires you and your child to feel empowered as you build lifelong confidence, resilience, and a deep sense of safety. Nurture these lessons together, knowing your connection will help your child thrive with assurance, courage, and love.

Suzanne T. Christian

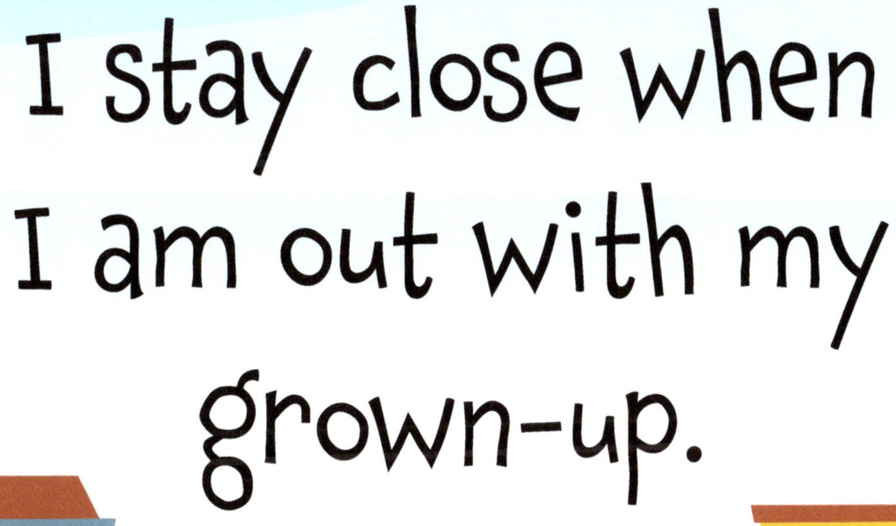

I stay close when
I am out with my
grown-up.

In the parking lot, I hold
my grown-up's hand.

At the park, I play
where my grown-up
can see me.

At the store, I stay
with my grown-up.

I do not go with someone I do not know.

If someone calls,
"Come here,"
I look for my grown-up.

If someone wants to help me, I ask my grown-up first.

I do not take treats from someone I do not know.

Before I go anywhere,
I ask my grown-up first.

If someone offers
me something,
I ask my grown-up
first.

NO

I use my listening ears when my grown-up says, "Stay near."

In a crowd, I hold my
grown-up's hand.

If someone I do not know talks to me, I stay close to my grown-up.

When we cross the street,
I hold my grown-up's hand.

I do not walk away to follow
a puppy, ball, or balloon.

When I want to go look
at something, I ask
my grown-up first.

I do not walk
away by myself.

Out and about, I stay
with my grown-up!

I Stay With MY GROWN-UP!

The End!

My Amazing Toddler Behavioral Series

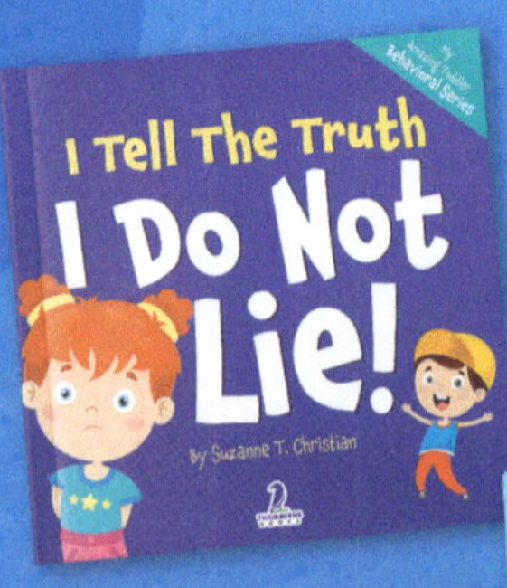

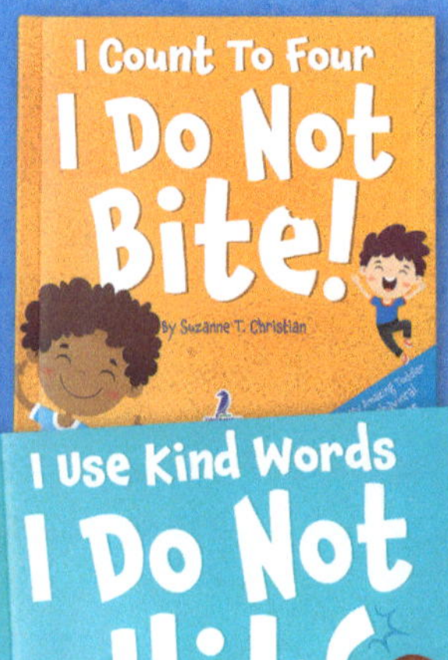

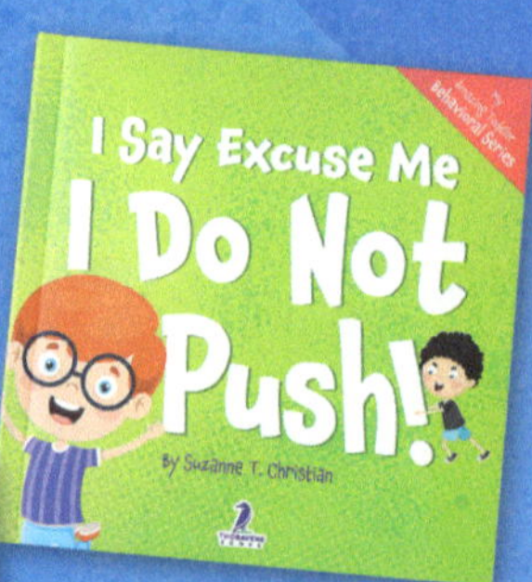

My Fingers Are For Tickling
I Do Not Pinch!
By Suzanne T. Christian

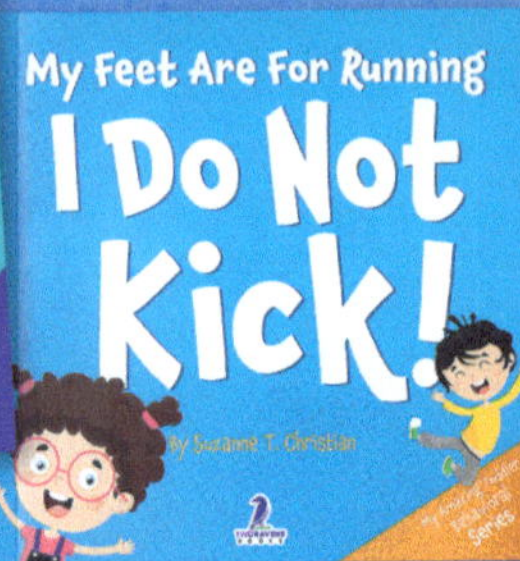

Check Out
Suzanne T. Christian's beloved series
'My Amazing Toddler Behavioral Series'.
Young readers are sure to enjoy!

Two Little Ravens

CHILDREN'S NON-FICTION BOOKS

Dear Amazing Reader,

Thank you for diving into **I Stay With My Grown-Up!** with me.
If this book touched your heart or made a difference for a
young reader, I'd be grateful if you could share your thoughts
in a review. Your feedback inspires my future work and helps
others discover the magic within these pages.

I'd love to hear from you directly if you have suggestions or
ideas for improving the book. Please feel free to reach out to
me at **suzanne.christian@tworavensbooks.com.** Your voice
counts, and I cherish it deeply.

With heartfelt gratitude,

www.ingramcontent.com/pod-product-compliance
Lightning Source LLC
Chambersburg PA
CBHW042135030726
47599CB00002B/476